MAKANDAL

The Black Messiah

by Frantz Derenoncourt Jr.

Illustrated by Eminence System

www.lfbookpublishing.com

Summary: An in depth account of the life of the Maroon leader, Makandal, who fought relentlessly to free Africans from French rule in Haiti.

ISBN-10: 0-9974925-3-8
ISBN-13: 978-0-9974925-3-8

Stay Connected with Frantz Derenoncourt, Jr. at www.thorobredbooks.com.

Special Thanks

Thank you to my ancestors for inspiring me
to write their memorable stories so that those
that have never heard the names of Makandal,
Boukman, Toussaint, Dessalines,
and many others may salute their efforts
and recognize them as heroes.

Also, this book would not have been possible
without the decades of study and research by
historian Mark Davis. Thank you for your website,
your novel, and the many email exchanges we've had.

Author's Note

It is impossible to do justice to such an important figure in history like Makandal. Especially when his life is shrouded in myth, legend, and hearsay. One of the many challenges in putting this book together was separating fact from legend in order to give as accurate an account of Makandal's life as possible. However, since most of his exploits were not recorded at the time it is impossible to write an official biography of his life. Many detailed parts of his life still remain unknown or not confirmed which opens the door to many theories and debates. The question of his missing hand is a perfect example. Some say that it was his hand that was missing, some say it was his whole arm. Some question that he was missing a limb at all. And if he was missing a limb, how did he lose it. Was it an accident at the sugar refining plant or was it harsh discipline from his slave master. Was he Muslim? Did he practice vodou? Even the spelling of his name is a hot topic...Makandal, Mackandal, or Macandal.

There are many questions that will be debated until the end of time. However, I didn't want the minor details to distract from the major impact that Makandal had in the freedom of enslaved black people worldwide. During Makandal's time, the French colony of Saint Domingue was the most profitable colony in the world and the treatment of enslaved Africans was one of the most severe. Makandal used his knowledge and leadership abilities to coordinate one the biggest liberation movements of the 18th century. He is credited with unifying the maroons, having them put their differences aside to fight for the greater good. His poison conspiracy network spanned from the maroons in the mountains, to the enslaved on the plantations, to the free blacks and possibly whites on the island. He was able to organize and communicate with all of them in an attempt to end the enslavement of his people.

In a time when the French colonists were preaching doctrine in an effort to convince the Africans that they were born to be slaves, Makandal is credited with breaking those mental chains of slavery using his knowledge of both Islam and Christianity.

Makandal was a revolutionary that should never be forgotten. My hope is that this book sparks those that are interested to look deeper into his movement and carry the torch forward.

*"Until The Lion Learns To Write,
Every Story Will Glorify The Hunter"*

—African Proverb

Based On A True Story

There was once a talented and gifted boy, the son of a village chief in Congo, Africa. It was well known in the village that this 12-year-old boy had advanced abilities such as reading and writing in his native language, Arabic.

This was something only a very small number of people in the area knew how to do. The boy was a masterful artist and would spend his days writing, painting, and playing musical instruments.

One day, the son's village was raided by slave traders. These men would storm into villages in Africa, kidnapping thousands of people and enslaving them. The boy and his friends had tried to escape the raid by running into the forest, but it was too late. The boy was captured.

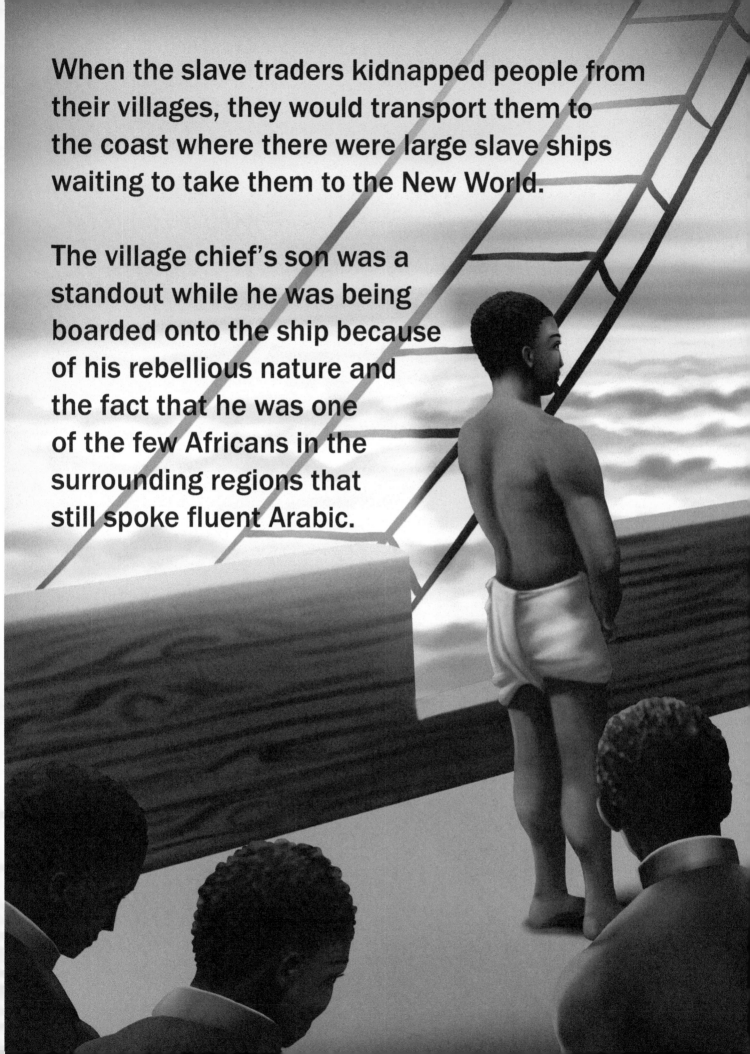

When the slave traders kidnapped people from their villages, they would transport them to the coast where there were large slave ships waiting to take them to the New World.

The village chief's son was a standout while he was being boarded onto the ship because of his rebellious nature and the fact that he was one of the few Africans in the surrounding regions that still spoke fluent Arabic.

Since the slave traders kidnapped him from a kingdom named Makanda, they named the boy Makandal. The journey to the New World was long and scary. But Makandal remained brave.

Makandal was led off of the slave ship,
and he stepped onto land for the first time
in over a month. He was told the name of his
New World was Saint Domingue, present-day Haiti.
Saint Domingue was a colony of France.

Makandal was an instant popular figure on the plantation. The other enslaved people were always in awe of his unique abilities. He was known for his wit and intelligence, and he raised the morale and confidence of all the enslaved Africans around him.

Makandal had become the plantation medicine man because of his vast knowledge of plants. He knew the healing effects of dozens of plants that grew on the island. People from plantations near and far came to him to be cured from different ailments and diseases. He was always happy to help.

Makandal loved telling the people on the plantation stories about his ancestors in Africa. People would always gather around to hear him speak. Makandal had taught himself how to read and speak the French language very quickly and started teaching the other enslaved people on the plantation. The slave masters did not like this because education of the slaves was strictly forbidden. They started keeping a close eye on him.

Now a young man at age 18, Makandal met an enslaved woman he liked and began to spend time with her. The only problem was that she worked in the slave master's house, and he would have to sneak over there to see her. When the slave master saw this, he became very angry and had Makandal captured and sentenced to 50 lashes with a bullwhip, which no person could survive.

While Makandal was receiving his punishment, he managed to break free from his shackles and escape into the mountains. He was hurt very badly, but this did not slow him down.

While in the mountains, Makandal joined a village of maroons. A maroon was a person who had escaped slavery. There were thousands of maroons in the mountains and dozens of maroon villages.

While in his village, Makandal began to speak out against the injustice of slavery. He said that slavery was not the reason for their existence. He preached that everyone was equal and deserved to be free, which was the opposite of what the French slave masters had told them. Makandal was able to unite all the different maroon tribes in the mountains with his message, which was to fight for one common goal: an end to the enslavement of their brothers and sisters on the plantation.

Makandal captured the attention of every enslaved person on the colony. Most of them had already accepted their fate as slaves, but Makandal gave them hope.

The maroons would usually band together at night and raid plantations for food, clothes, and other supplies they needed to survive in the mountains. They would also use the raids as an opportunity to recruit new maroons.

Makandal was always one of the most fearless leaders of the maroons, and he was dashing and daring in his conquests. His exploits during the raids would only add to his legend.

During one of the raids, Makandal was caught by the slave masters and locked up in a jail on the plantation. The penalty for raids against the French slave owners was death.

But when the slave masters went to Makandal's cell to carry out his sentence, he was gone. He had escaped again.

Drawing on his experience performing successful raids on the plantations, Makandal came up with a plan to defeat the French slave masters and free the island of slavery once and for all. In order for his plan to work properly he would need the help of the gens de couleur (free people of color) in Saint Domingue who had access to resources he needed in order to win the battle.

However, he could not convince them to join his revolution.

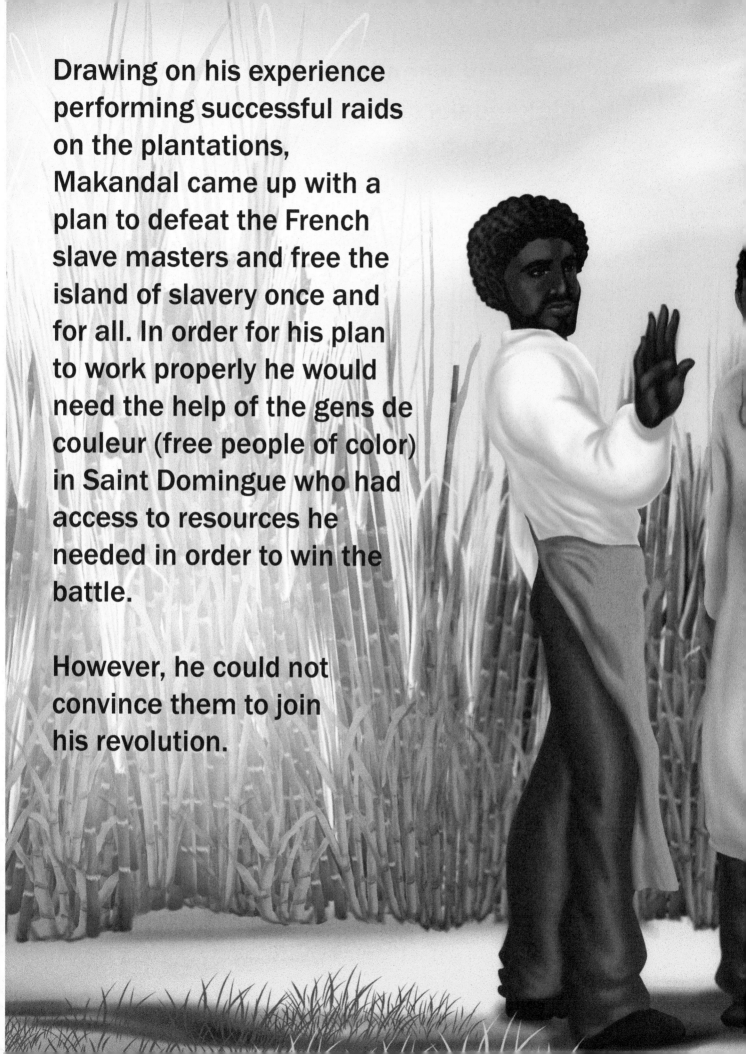

Even though he did not get any support from the
gens de couleur, Makandal did not give up on his
plan to end the enslavement of his people.
He decided to fight his enemy using what he
knew best, plants. Just as he knew how to create
medicine from plants, he also knew how to make
poison. He formed a plan to make thousands
of portions of poison using the native plants
in the mountains and distribute them to his
vast network of people on the plantations.

They would put the poison in the slave masters' food and drinks. After the slaveowners had fallen sick from the poison, he would attack the plantations with his maroon army.

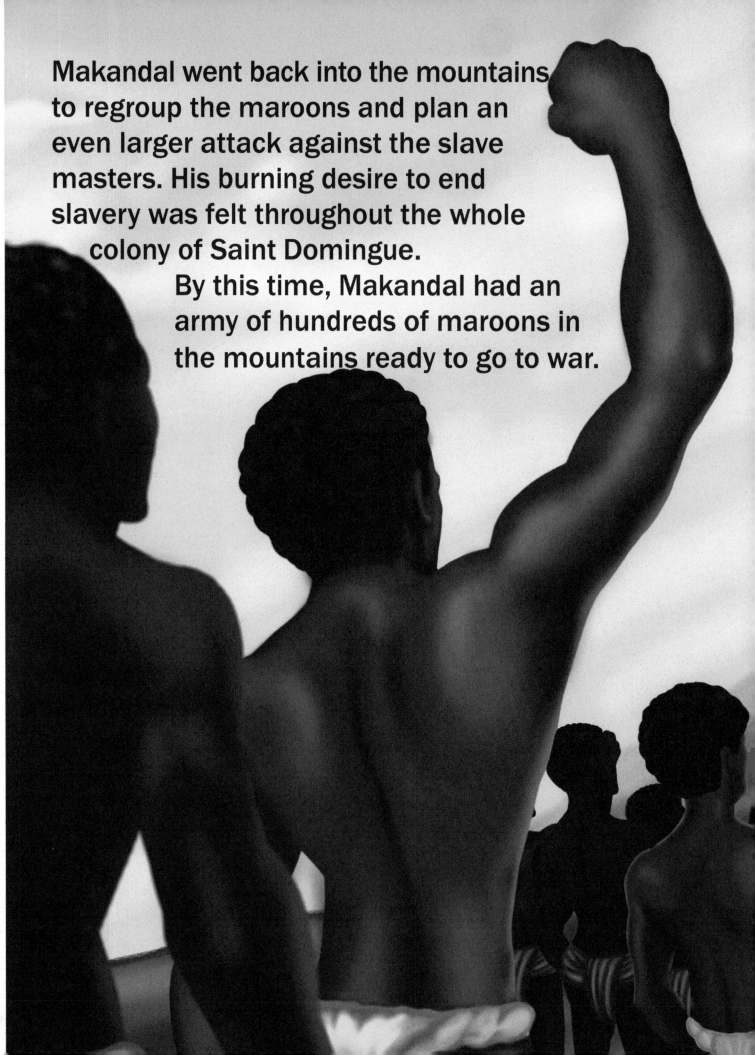

Makandal went back into the mountains to regroup the maroons and plan an even larger attack against the slave masters. His burning desire to end slavery was felt throughout the whole colony of Saint Domingue.

By this time, Makandal had an army of hundreds of maroons in the mountains ready to go to war.

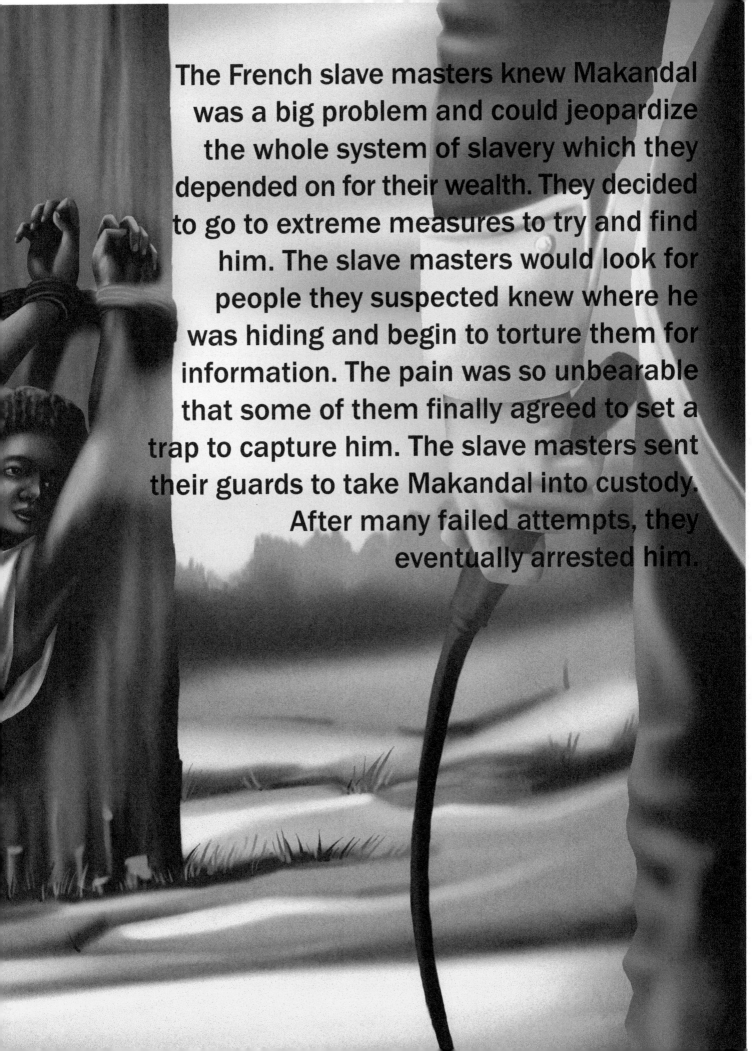

The French slave masters knew Makandal was a big problem and could jeopardize the whole system of slavery which they depended on for their wealth. They decided to go to extreme measures to try and find him. The slave masters would look for people they suspected knew where he was hiding and begin to torture them for information. The pain was so unbearable that some of them finally agreed to set a trap to capture him. The slave masters sent their guards to take Makandal into custody. After many failed attempts, they eventually arrested him.

The slave masters attempted to make an example of Makandal, so they tied him to a stake in front of thousands of people in the town square. As he was set to be executed, Makandal proclaimed loudly that slavery would end, and the black people of Saint Domingue would rise up to rule the island themselves.

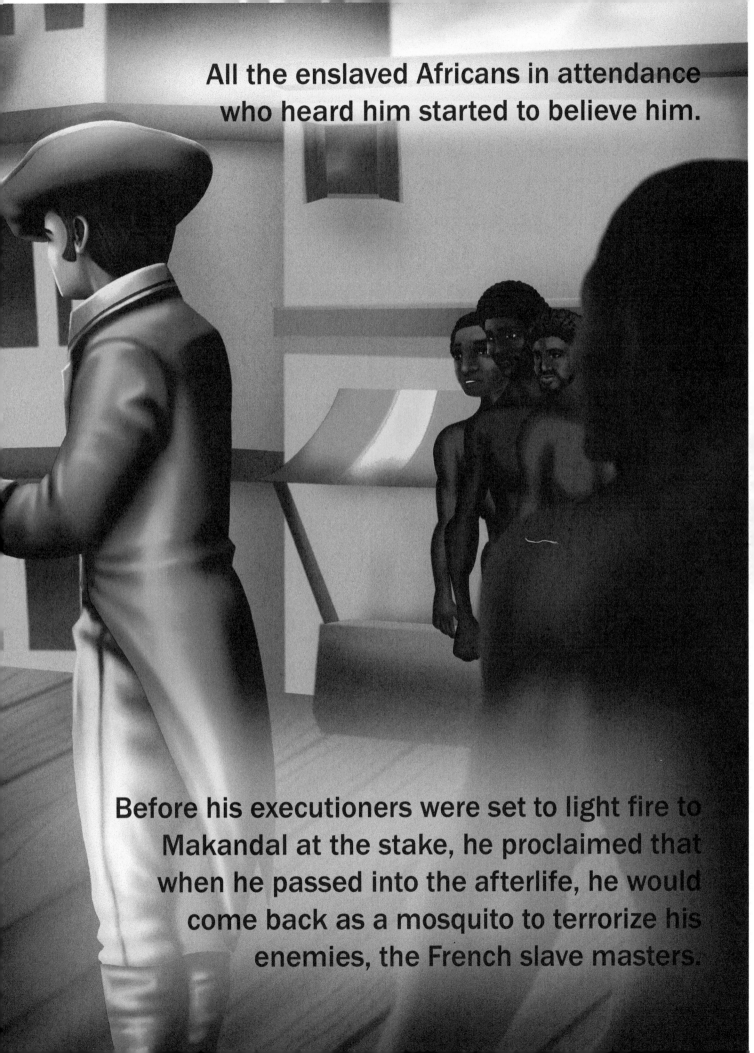

All the enslaved Africans in attendance who heard him started to believe him.

Before his executioners were set to light fire to Makandal at the stake, he proclaimed that when he passed into the afterlife, he would come back as a mosquito to terrorize his enemies, the French slave masters.

There are many different versions of what happened that day on January 20, 1758. Some say that he broke free from his bonds and escaped into the mountains while some say he perished at the stake. Either way, Makandal was never heard from again.

Thirty-three years after Makandal's death (or disappearance), a maroon named Dutty Boukman held a secret ceremony at the same site where Makandal had made some of his inspiring speeches. The site is known as Bois Caïman, the starting place of the Haitian Revolution. That victory made Haiti the first black republic in the history of the world on January 1, 1804.

One of the many reasons that Haitian rebels were victorious in their war for independence was the rapid spread of yellow fever that claimed the lives of over twenty thousand European soldiers. The deadly virus was spread by an infestation of mosquitoes. To this day, many Haitian people believe the infestation of mosquitoes was the reincarnation of the African village chief's son, Makandal.

Bio

Frantz Derenoncourt, Jr. is a first generation Haitian-American born and raised in East Flatbush, Brooklyn, NY. After very humble beginnings he attended Virginia State University in Petersburg, VA where he majored in Business Management and soon after moved to the nations capitol, Washington, DC. After working a few 9 to 5 jobs around town, Frantz fell in love with the real estate industry and found success as a real estate sales associate and real estate investor.

As a child growing up in Brooklyn in the early 80s, Frantz was often picked on for being Haitian. Teachers could never pronounce his name correctly and the students would always have a cruel Haitian joke on hand. At times, he felt ashamed to be Haitian until he started reading about Haitian history. The fact that his little country accomplished something that no other nation had accomplished at that time gave him a tremendous sense of pride. He started reading everything he could get his hands on in regards to the Haitian Revolution and relaying the stories to his son, Chase. Chase was just as excited as Frantz was and it was then that he realized that this fascinating story needs to be told in a way that even a 2nd grade reader can appreciate the accomplishment of his ancestors. Frantz's fervor for teaching Haitian history birthed his first book, *"Haiti: The First Black Republic,"* which went on to receive global recognition. *"Haiti: The First Black Republic,"* in a short period of time, garnered Frantz Derenoncourt Jr. a vast following, hungry for knowledge on Haitian history. One of Frantz's greatest accomplishments was being featured in *Essence Magazine*, resulting from the momentous wave his literary work created.

In part to the demand of Frantz's gift to articulate Haitian history, and his desire to tell the whole story of the Haitian Revolution, "Makandal: The Black Messiah" was birthed. This is the latest, in a series of books that Frantz Derenoncourt Jr. will create to empower all black and brown people alike, worldwide.

To learn more about Frantz Derenoncourt, Jr., please visit www.thorobredbooks.com.

Mission Statement

My mission for this book is to establish a sense of pride in the black youth all over the world. I also aim to tell the stories of success and victory of a people against impossible odds.

I also write to let the world know that if you're a person of color from Haiti, Dominican Republic, Cuba, the United States or any other nation, all of our ancestors came from the same place. A win for one of us, is a win for all of us.

CPSIA information can be obtained
at www.ICGtesting.com
Printed in the USA
BVOW05*2306290117
474729BV00003B/5/P